AVENGERS PRIME

AVENGERS PRIME. Contains material originally published in magazine form as AVENGERS PRIME #1-5. First printing 2011. Hardcover ISBN# 978-0-7851-4725-1. Softcover ISBN# 978-0-7851-4726-8. Published by MARVEL WORLDWIDE, INC., a subsidiary of MARVEL ENTERTAINMENT, LLC. OFFICE OF PUBLICATION: 135 West 50th Street, New York, NY 10020. Copyright © 2010 and 2011 Marvel Characters, Inc. All rights reserved. Hardcover: $24.99 per copy in the U.S. and $27.99 in Canada (GST #R127032852). Softcover: $16.99 per copy in the U.S. and $18.99 in Canada (GST #R127032852). Canadian Agreement #40668537. All characters featured in this issue and the distinctive names and likenesses thereof, and all related indicia are trademarks of Marvel Characters, Inc. No similarity between any of the names, characters, persons, and/or institutions in this magazine with those of any living or dead person or institution is intended, and any such similarity which may exist is purely coincidental. **Printed in the U.S.A.** ALAN FINE, EVP - Office of the President, Marvel Worldwide, Inc. and EVP & CMO Marvel Characters B.V.; DAN BUCKLEY, Publisher & President - Print, Animation & Digital Divisions; JOE QUESADA, Chief Creative Officer; JIM SOKOLOWSKI, Chief Operating Officer; DAVID BOGART, SVP of Business Affairs & Talent Management; TOM BREVOORT, SVP of Publishing; C.B. CEBULSKI, SVP of Creator & Content Development; DAVID GABRIEL, SVP of Publishing Sales & Circulation; MICHAEL PASCIULLO, SVP of Brand Planning & Communications; JIM O'KEEFE, VP of Operations & Logistics; DAN CARR, Executive Director of Publishing Technology; JUSTIN F. GABRIE, Director of Publishing & Editorial Operations; SUSAN CRESPI, Editorial Operations Manager; ALEX MORALES, Publishing Operations Manager; STAN LEE, Chairman Emeritus. For information regarding advertising in Marvel Comics or on Marvel.com, please contact Ron Stern, VP of Business Development, at rstern@marvel.com. For Marvel subscription inquiries, please call 800-217-9158. **Manufactured between 2/21/2011 and 3/21/2011 (hardcover), and 2/21/2011 and 9/19/2011 (softcover), by R.R. DONNELLEY, INC., SALEM, VA, USA.**

10 9 8 7 6 5 4 3 2 1

AVENGERS PRIME

WRITER	**BRIAN MICHAEL BENDIS**
PENCILER	**ALAN DAVIS**
INKER	**MARK FARMER**
COLORIST	**JAVIER RODRIGUEZ**
LETTERER	**CHRIS ELIOPOULOS**
ASSOCIATE EDITOR	**LAUREN SANKOVITCH**
EDITOR	**TOM BREVOORT**

Collection Editor: JENNIFER GRÜNWALD
Editorial Assistants: JAMES EMMETT & JOE HOCHSTEIN
Assistant Editors: ALEX STARBUCK & NELSON RIBEIRO
Editor, Special Projects: MARK D. BEAZLEY
Senior Editor, Special Projects: JEFF YOUNGQUIST
Senior Vice President of Sales: DAVID GABRIEL
Book Design: JEFF POWELL

Editor in Chief: AXEL ALONSO
Chief Creative Officer: JOE QUESADA
Publisher: DAN BUCKLEY
Executive Producer: ALAN FINE

EARTH'S MIGHTIEST HEROES, UNITED AGAINST A COMMON THREAT! ON THAT DAY THE AVENGERS WERE BORN, TO FIGHT FOES THAT NO SINGLE HERO COULD WITH-STAND!

SIEGE: AFTERMATH
AVENGERS
PRIME

NORMAN OSBORN'S SIEGE IS OVER AND THE REUNITED AVENGERS WERE TRIUMPHANT. STEVE ROGERS, THE MAN WHO WAS CAPTAIN AMERICA, IS NOW IN CHARGE OF THE UNITED STATES' SECURITY.

BUT ALL THIS WAS NOT WITHOUT COST. THE GREAT CITY OF ASGARD HAS FALLEN.

DIGITAL FINGERPRINT LOCK SEQUENCE.

3.8 DESIGN.

3.8 DESIGN.

YEAH, YEAH... I REMEMBER NOW.

AH. THERE WE GO.

THE SELF REPAIR KIT.

I DO LOVE ME SOMETIMES.

ACTUALLY, MY KINGDOM FOR A COFFEE.

OH, UH, HI.

YOU WOULDN'T HAPPEN TO BE A BARISTA...WOULD YOU?

My sincere apologies for disturbing your evening.

Would any of you be able to tell me where I am?

I am an ally of Lord Thor. I need help.

Can you tell me where I am?

UGH!

YOU'RE AN ALLY OF THE LORD THOR?

SON OF ODIN?

YES. ENGLISH. GOOD.

THERE WAS SOME SORT OF AN ACCIDENT--

EAT HIM!

AAGGH!

GAAGGH!

IT'S ONLY A MIDGARD RAT!

HOW MANY WILL IT TAKE FOR YOU TO STOP THIS?

2

UH, HI.

MY NAME IS TONY STARK.

IRON MAN.

RING ANY BELLS?

KINDA SORTA FAMOUS WHERE I'M FROM...

THOUGHT MAYBE IT TRANSLATED OUTSIDE MY...

YOU DIDN'T HAPPEN TO SEE THOR AROUND HERE?

HE'S A PERSONAL FRIEND.

THOR? GOD OF THUNDER? EASY ON THE EYES?

THOR?

NO? NOTHING.

OKAY... THEN... YOU WOULD DARE STRIKE A WIZARD?!

YOU WOULD DARE?!

I'M SORRY. ARE YOU STUPID? OR DO YOU THINK *US* STUPID?

HMM. CAN I GET BACK TO YOU ON THAT ONE?

YOU SURRENDER THEN?

UM... TECHNICALLY.

BUT ONLY BECAUSE I'M OVERPOWERED AND COMPLETELY SURROUNDED.

GOOD MORTAL.

"MORTAL."

WOULD YOU MIND TELLING ME WHERE I AM AND WHO I AM SURRENDERING TO?

UH-HUH. THEN LET'S START WITH THE *"WHERE I ACTUALLY AM"* PART.

AND PLEASE DON'T SAY ANYTHING LIKE--

ONE COULD SAY THAT ANY SURRENDER IS, IN FACT, A SURRENDER TO ONESELF.

YOU'RE ON A PATH OF YOUR OWN CHOOSING.

LIKE THAT.

NO, SEE, I AM ACTUALLY NOT ON A PATH OF MY OWN CHOOSING.

I WAS WITH YOUR LORD THOR AND WE ACCIDENTALLY WERE TRANSPORTED TO--

TO ANSWER THAT QUESTION YOU HAVE TO ASK ANOTHER.

WHERE IS ASGARD?

YOU KNOW WHERE IT IS.

IT'S ON EARTH.

ASGARD IS ON MIDGARD?

YES.

I--IS THAT EVEN POSSIBLE?

IT IS.

THAT I--I HAD NOT HEARD.

WHY?

DOES THAT SEEM NATURAL TO YOU?

THERE ARE NINE REALMS. NINE. NINE WORLDS OF ASGARD'S RULE.

NINE!

BUT NOW ONE OF THEM, ASGARD ITSELF, THE GOLDEN JEWEL OF ODIN'S CORRUPT, MALIGNANT KINGDOM, RESIDES IN THE SOWHEAP OF THE UNIVERSE.

MIDGARD.

AND NOW THESE SEA RATS ARE ALLOWED TO ENTER OUR REALM UNATTENDED?

THOR'S FRIENDS ARE ALLOWED HERE TO--

TO WHAT?

TO MOCK US?

TO PILLAGE US LIKE THEY DO THEMSELVES?

WHY?

BECAUSE YOU AND YOUR FATHER ALLOWED IT.

AND NOW LOOK WHAT HAS HAPPENED.

DOES THAT SEEM AT ALL RIGHT TO YOU?

IT IS THE WAY THINGS ARE NOW.

BECAUSE YOU ALLOWED IT.

DON'T SPEAK IN CIRCLES! TELL ME TRUE... WHAT HAS HAPPENED?

WHERE ARE WE?

THE REALMS HAVE FALLEN INTO DARK TIMES.

ALL THE VILLAGERS THINK-- IT FEELS AS IF THEY'VE BLED INTO EACH OTHER.

ON TOP OF EACH OTHER.

OUR BLUE SKIES HAVE BURNT TO ORANGE. OUR--OUR DAYS HAVE TURNED TO NIGHT.

BLOOD FLOWS IN EVERY RIVER AND LAKE.

THERE IS NO DIFFERENCE BETWEEN WHAT WAS TRULY GOOD AND WHAT WAS NOT.

HOW DID THIS HAPPEN?

YOU DESTROYED THE BALANCE OF THE REALMS AND, IN DOING SO, YOU RIPPED YOUR FATHER'S EMPIRE INTO A NIGHTMARE.

THIS IS NOT MY FAULT!

I DON'T EVEN KNOW WHAT THIS IS!

OF COURSE THIS IS THOR'S FAULT.

THOR, ODIN, LOKI, THEIR GAMES. THEIR MACHINATIONS!

EVEN IN DEATH, ODIN'S MYOPIC RULE BLANKETS US IN FILTH AND DESPAIR.

I DO NOT TRUST YOU, WITCH.

I WANT TO SEE THIS NIGHTMARE FOR MYSELF.

IF THIS WORLD IS BROKEN, I WILL FIX IT.

IF YOU WANT TO HELP... HELP.

BUT DO NOT STAY MY HAND ANY LONGER.

THE OINTMENTS WILL HEAL YOU QUICKLY. IF THOU STAYEST CALM AND DRY.

BUT I FEAR YOU WILL DO NEITHER.

I HAVE TO FIND MY FRIENDS.

FFMARRGH!

SO NOW, WE HAVE SOMETHING THAT WILL HURT THE HOUSE OF ODIN.

OH, YOU GOTTA BE KIDDING ME.

I CAN'T HELP YOU. ALL I KNOW IS THIS VILLAGE.

THANK YOU FOR YOUR KINDNESS.

YOU SHOULD LISTEN TO THE ENCHANTRESS, LORD THOR.

YOU...

#3 NYCC VARIANT BY JIM CHEUNG &
SKOTTIE YOUNG

DO YOU KNOW WHERE WE ARE?

READING, PENNSYLVANIA.

WHAT?

I WAS TRYING TO BE FUNNY.

TRY HARDER.

IT'S ONE OF THE NINE REALMS.

I DON'T KNOW MY NINE REALMS VERY WELL.

DID I SAY THANKS BEFORE?

YOU ACTUALLY DID. WHICH WAS A PLEASANT SURPRISE.

DON'T BE SNIPPY, WE'RE HAVING KIND OF A BONDING MOMENT.

YOU READY?

ALL I NEED IS AN OUTLET AND AN AC ADAPTOR.

YOU USED THAT LINE DURING THE WHOLE KORVAC THING.

AND MANY TIMES SINCE.

I'M NOT CHARGED AND I'M OFFLINE.

THIS IS JUST A SUIT OF ARMOR FOR NOW.

WHERE WE ARE...THAT MIGHT BE ALL YOU NEED.

AND I HAVE MY ROLLER SKATES IF WE, YOU KNOW, FIND ANY PAVEMENT.

HOP ON.

THERE'S GOT TO BE ANOTHER HORSE RUNNING AROUND HERE SOMEWHERE.

HOP ON! LET'S GO.

ANY EXCUSE TO GET ME TO HOLD YOU.

YOU SEE RIGHT THROUGH ME.

WHERE'S THOR?

DON'T KNOW EXACTLY.

I'M FOLLOWING THE LIGHTNING.

THIS IS MAGETH. SHE'S A FRIEND. SHE GAVE US SHELTER.

MY--MY APOLOGIES, FAIR MAIDEN.

MY FORTUNES HAVE BEEN AFOUL LATELY.

WHAT HAPPENED TO YOU, THOR?

WHERE'S MJOLNIR?

SHE TOOK IT?

WHO WAS IT?

HELA.

OH, GODS.

THE GOD OF--?

THE GODDESS OF DEATH.

WONDERFUL.

AND SHE JUST FOUND YOU HERE, JUMPED YOU, AND TOOK YOUR HAMMER?

HOW WOULD SHE EVEN KNOW YOU WERE HERE?

WE CAME HERE BY COMPLETE ACCIDENT!

SHE WASN'T ALONE.

THE ENCHANTRESS WAS THERE.

TO WATCH ME FALL.

HOW CAN THAT BE, LORD THOR?

"AT FIRST I THOUGHT PERHAPS HELA WAS JUST A TRICK.

"AN APPARITION.

"A TRICK OF THE EYE BROUGHT TO LIFE BY THE ENCHANTRESS."

BUT HELA'S POWER WAS TOO GREAT. I FELL TO HER STEEL.

4

ARE WE WORRIED THAT YOU DON'T HAVE YOUR HAMMER?

THE ENCHANTMENT SAYS NO ONE CAN LIFT IT BUT MYSELF.

BUT IT WAS TAKEN AWAY FROM YOU.

YES.

IT IS A DEEP CONCERN, BUT WE MUST HAVE FAITH.

ARE YOU PLANNING SOMETHING?

IS THAT WHAT YOU'RE DOING?

THERE IS MUCH TO CONTEMPLATE.

WE WAIT FOR DAYLIGHT. THEN WE WILL DISCOVER THE NEW TRUTH OF THIS COUNTRYSIDE.

ARE YOU PRAYING?

IN A WAY.

SHOULD WE ALL PRAY?

I CANNOT SEE HOW IT COULD HURT.

I MEANT TO SAY, THOR...

I AM SORRY ABOUT ASGARD.

AND I'M SORRY ABOUT YOUR BROTHER.

I'M NOT SURE HOW I FEEL ABOUT LOKI'S DEMISE.

HE BROUGHT IT ON HIMSELF AS WE ALWAYS KNEW HE WOULD.

WELL THEN, I'M SORRY ABOUT YOUR BROTHER IF *YOU'RE* SORRY ABOUT YOUR BROTHER.

BUT IF YOU'RE MAD AT HIM FOR CREATING THE SITUATION THAT PULLED DOWN ASGARD AND BROUGHT US HERE...THAN I AM TOO.

JUST SAYIN'.

YOU KNOW...

IF NOT FOR THE FACT THAT WE MAY BE *DEAD*, AND WE DON'T KNOW WHERE WE *ARE*, AND THE *GOBLINS* AND THE *DRAGONS* AND THE *ELVES*...

OR THE FACT THAT THERE'S NO *BATHROOM*...

THIS IS ACTUALLY KIND OF *NICE*.

YOU WERE ASLEEP FROM WORLD WAR TWO UP UNTIL THE DAY BEFORE YESTERDAY.

WHAT DO *YOU* NEED A VACATION FOR?

THAT'S TRUE, TOO.

HEY, I'VE BEEN MEANING TO ASK YOU...

I'VE NEVER BEEN ON A REAL VACATION.

I GUESS THIS IS AS CLOSE AS I'M LIKELY TO GET.

IS THIS GOING TO START ANOTHER FIGHT?

REMEMBER HELLCAT?

YES.

PATSY WALKER. SHE WAS AN AVENGER FOR TEN MINUTES.

I REMEMBER.

YOU GUYS EVER HOOK UP?

WHAT?

YOU WILL TELL ME WHAT YOU *KNOW* OF THIS TWISTED REALM!

YOU WILL TELL ME HOW YOU GOT HERE AND HOW LONG YOU HAVE BEEN HERE--

#5 VARIANT BY ARTHUR ADAMS &
MORRY HOLLOWELL

THE END.